Printed by Kiyanni B., Write It Out Publishing, LLC. in the United States of America.

Write It Out Publishing LLC

Virginia Beach, Virginia

Writeitoutpublishing.com

ISBN: 979-8-9874539-6-4

Book Cover Illustrator: Maurice Rogers

Editor: Renee Johnson & Tamira K. Butler-Likely

First printing, (e-book or paperback) August 9, 2023

Jarius Hillman

Richmond, VA 23223

jarius32.jh@gmail.com

JARIUS HILLMAN

MODERN DAY PRIESTS

A Practical Guide For New Covenant Priesthood

Write It Out
PUBLISHING, LLC

VIRGINIA BEACH, VA

JARIUS HILLMAN

■ ■ ■

MODERN DAY PRIESTS

A Practical Guide For New Covenant Priesthood

Contents

To my Transformation Church VA family, thank you for accepting and grooming me to accept me. Thank you to my fiance for pushing and believing in me. Thank you to Jesus Christ for saving and bringing my heart alive!

As I'm typing this, I'm in shock that I'm doing so. For one, I've never seen myself as an author, or as we would say in Christendom, a scribe, and two, to write on this topic of priesthood. However, what I know for sure is I feel the burden of God to write this and to shed light on this word that is on the cover. Matter of fact, it's not just a word, but it's a LIFE-STYLE. It's a word that has been thrown around, but it's one of a devoted life of continual sacrifice. A life of consecration. A life that has a standard attached to it that consists of informing, service, and habitual fellowship with God our Father.

The definition of a standard, according to Merriam-Webster, "something set up and established by authority as a rule for the measure of quantity, weight, extent, value, or quality." In the chapters to come, I will explain in greater detail what was just mentioned, but before that is done, let me touch on the reason this book was written and published. This book is a tool for the understanding of who all new covenant believers are and how we're meant to live as believers, along with our authority as God's children through Jesus Christ. Over the entire year of 2022, the Lord pulled on my heart to discover the origin and description of a Priest. And while this was being done, I realized how little the body of Christ knows of this subject, but most importantly how priesthood is still relevant to this day! I believe the Spirit of God is awakening the hearts of those who are burdened with the mandate of the Priests of old, and as they once did, instruct the people in the Lord's way of doing and living a life for Him.

I believe that the hearts of the Priests have been grieving without knowledge of why they feel the way they do. My prayer is that this will give the body of Christ a level setting. To bring everyone on the same level, whether you're new in your faith walk, or have been walking with Jesus a long time. This tool will not only have the history of the Priest, but its description according to the Bible and practical ways to carry out this standard that God set. Every bit of teaching you will read will come from scripture and can be traced to a specific text out of the sixty-six books, because an ignorant Christian is one that can be twisted and lacks accountability. Without further ado, let's explore!

DEFINITIONS OF A PRIEST

"Tell all the skilled and talented people whom I have endowed with a spirit of wisdom, that they are to make Aaron's garments to sanctify him and set him apart to serve as a priest for Me."
-Exodus 28:3 AMP

Before we take a look at the verse above and dissect it, I have to talk about Sonship first. This is not gender phobic but rather speaking to the biblical principle, so if you're offended, take it up with God. Sonship is explained excellently in Galatians 4:4–7, speaking of how Jesus was born on Earth under the law to free us from the law so we could be adopted as sons of God. We are children of God before we're ever a priest, a pastor, a mother, brother, so on and so forth. Understanding this is influential so we know that as God's children, He loves us, protects us, provides for us, and leads us as a good Father should. If the idea of God being a good Father has caused a discomfort to rise within you or make you squirm, then I urge you to talk to a seasoned fellow Christian, a therapist, and pray because what we have stumbled upon is a wound from our earthly fathers.

Unfortunately, our view of our earthly fathers are reflected on our heavenly Father, which will distort our view of Him being good. Heal Priest! Heal so you can fully identify yourself as God's beloved and come into full awareness of your purpose and authority. Now, that our foundation is being built from identifying as a son of God, we can actually begin talking about the definition of a Priest. Stemming from the verse, we see that Priests are to serve God and are set apart for this service. Pay attention to that last part, as it will come up again in a later chapter. Let's look a little deeper to get a better picture of the office of a Priest.

If we look in Numbers 18:1–7 and 20, we see that the duties of the Priests were to make sacrifices on the behalf of the nation to God for the atonement of sins. Priests directly minister to God on behalf of the people; you can view them as the middleman between God and His people. The Priests stood in the gap for the nation of Israel so God's judgment wouldn't come on the behalf of theirs and the nation's sins, both knowingly and unknowingly. Sticking with scriptures 1–7 we see that the Priests were the only ones allowed to go into the tent of meeting which is the Holy place and the High Priests the Holies of Holies. This was due to God designating them to do so, but they also had to be consecrated, or else they would die there too. Fun fact: the Priests had bells on the hem of their garments so the people would know when they entered and exited the Holies of Holies but Jewish tradition states they placed a rope on them in case they died in there to pull them out.

The Bible tells us that the Priests bore the guilt, the iniquity, and sins of the nation and themselves, which if we can recall, Jesus did the same on Calvary. But let me not get too far ahead. Priests also were teachers of the law and distinguishers of Holy and common, as well as clean and unclean, according to Leviticus 10:10–11, which speaks of the Priests teaching God's people His statutes and knowing what is of His nature. I'll expand on this more, but to pull this altogether, this will be the definition of a Priest that we will use as we travel together. A Priest is someone who is the mediator between God and His people, who teaches them His ways, and ministers or serves Him.

PRIESTS OF OLD

"The Levites obeyed your word and guarded your covenant. They were more loyal to you than their own parents. They ignored their relatives and did not acknowledge their own children. [10] They teach your regulations to Jacob; they give your instructions to Israel. They present incense before you and offer whole burnt offerings on the altar."

- Deut. 33:9–10 NLT

The history of the Priest is extensive and is mainly discussed in the book of Exodus. It is elaborated, on or mentioned within Leviticus, Numbers, Deuteronomy, 1st & 2nd Samuel, and 2nd Chronicles, to name a few, that discuss roles and duties. Although the descriptions derive from these and other books of the Bible, it's in Genesis that we see the origin, and it's not where the typical conversation is started. I believe we see the first functions of the Priest, or foreshadowing if you will, come between Cain and Abel in their sacrifices made to God in Genesis 4:2–5. Reason being is we just read how the Priests offered sacrifices for the atonement of sins and ministered to God. In these sets of scriptures, although it doesn't mention sin atonement, we see the offerings they each presented to God.

Now, before anyone tries to call me a false teacher, let's look at definitions of each word (as you can tell definitions are important). Sacrifice is defined in Merriam-Webster as, "an act of offering to a deity something precious." An offering or offer is defined in Merriam-Webster as, "is something presented as an act of worship or devotion." So, we see that both words are acts of presentation, but let's look a little further.

The Hebrew word for Priests is "Kohanim" and they presented "Korbonat" or sacrifices/offerings to God. The root of "korban" means to draw close to, so sacrifices were not only used for atonement of sin, but to honor and be close to God. Korban is both offering and sacrifice! A bit of a rabbit hole, but all to verify that Cain and Abel were a foreshadowing of what was to come by giving offerings as an act of adoration.

Before going any further, let me make this crystal clear, ALL PRIESTS ARE WORSHIPPERS! The number one job, above everything else, was to minister unto God, which we can interpret as worship. It looks different for all, but to help the person reading this book, worship is giving your time, your attention, action, focus, etc. to a person, place, or thing, but for the believer that should be the Lord. Priests were/are the example of a life that's submitted to the Lord. The example of how to reach for the Lord, to be sensitive to His spirit, and to sit before His face as sons. Priests absolutely adore the presence of God. We even see the sons of Korah in Psalm 84:10 say they would rather be a doorkeeper in the house of God than in the tent of the wicked because they knew the joy, pleasures, and freedom of just being near Him.

Worship is a PIVOTAL point of the Priest's office. The first mention of a Priest is in Genesis 14:18–20, by the name of a man named Melchizedek, who was both a king and Priest of God. We don't know much about him other than him being recognized as a Priest of the most high God and blessing Abraham after his victory in the name of the Most High. Diving more into origins, the Priests came from the tribe of Levi, who was the son of Jacob (Israel) and Leah and his name means to unite or join together (Gen. 29:34). This is key because Priests also gather the people so they can all worship God together on the day of atonement and to hear what His instructions are for them.

Skipping ahead in the Word, we see the first establishment of the Priest through Aaron and his sons who were descendants of Levi. Referencing Exodus 28 again, we see the Lord specifically called Aaron and his sons to be his Priests and to be in charge of the Levites which were to help with work for the tent of meeting. For my Bible nerds and theologians, this is also spoken of in Leviticus 8 and Numbers 3. The reason why God chose Aaron and his sons is because Aaron was beside Moses and was used as a mouthpiece for God as well while the Israelites were still in Egypt.

Due to him speaking to Israel on the behalf of God, witnessing the miracles that God had done, and seeing first hand all of what He could do, Aaron knew God's character. He knew exactly how God felt about injustice, oppression, etc. as well as knowing God as a comforter, deliverer, provider, and miracle worker. With this knowledge, he would be able to teach the nation God's ways by His instructions from Moses, as well as experience. Keep this in mind when we get to the chapter about the enemies to the Priests. From them being appointed and set apart, the priesthood began to do the duties given to them, along with the other Levites as well as raise up those to take their place.

Another important piece to mention is that in Deuteronomy 18:1–2, God announces that the tribe of Levi (the Priests and other Levites), wouldn't receive a physical inheritance, but He would be their inheritance, and with the food offerings that were presented would be their food too. These Priests also served as judges to the nation of Israel in times of decision and even war when other nations would come against them. One of the major reasons Priests were so important is because they, along with prophets, were who were used to remind the people of God's history with them, as well as His character and thoughts.

This is important because after Joshua had taken the nation into the Promised Land and eventually had died, the generation after had no connection to God and what He had done for them (Judges 2:10). This lack of remembrance of God is what put the nation into so much sin to the point that God would only be with the judges He set, and as long as that judge was living they wouldn't be overwhelmed. After the judge had died, Israel would go back to their sinful ways following idols, and doing detestable things. During these times, we see the Priests are unfaithful and though they sacrificed to the Lord, their hearts were not for Him, and due these continual actions, the word of the Lord in those days were very rare. One thing is for certain, our God will always raise up someone who will be after His own heart to be a solution and restore His ways to His people.

We see that when the Prophet Samuel is born in 1 Samuel. Samuel is born from Hannah, whose womb was shut, but the Lord opened it up once she said she would dedicate the baby to do the Lord's work. Once born, he's given over to the High Priest, at that time, Eli, whose sons were also Priests doing detestable things in the temple. Due to this, Eli receives a word that his sons will die along with his bloodline and God will raise him up a faithful Priest that will do all that the Lord desires, and because of this establish their family to be Priests alongside kings forever (1 Samuel

2:34–35).

Theologians have different answers of who this Priest may be, between it being Samuel, the Priest whom David appointed whose name is Zadok, or even it being Jesus, but nevertheless what we can agree on is after Eli and his sons died, the priesthood was restored along with a nation that lived for God and did His will. From this, birthed the priesthood that most people know or hear of which is David's organizing of the Priests in the temple. This is where Zadok comes in because he helped David organize the Priests, as well as the rest of the Levites, and what sprung from this were Priests that resumed their duties and had hands in politics.

Fun fact: Jeremiah the Prophet was also a Priest according to Jeremiah 1:1, and we can't prove it, but Samuel did Priestly duties under Eli the High Priest (stay tuned, we're going to connect this later). With all this information about the Priests of the Old Testament, let's now move into where the Priests are in the New Testament.

NEW TESTAMENT PRIESTS

"But you are a chosen race, a royal priesthood, a holy nation, a people for God's own possession, so that you may proclaim the excellencies of Him who has called you out of darkness into His marvelous light;"

- 1 Peter 2:9 NASB

While Priests in the New Testament did the same duties, they were vastly different in their reverence for the Lord. Just to add to how different the sensitivity and love for God was, from the last book of the Old Testament (Malachi), to the first book of the New Testament (Matthew), the Lord did not utter a word to anyone for 400 years. This was supposed to be a time where they sought the Lord and studied His law, but the opposite was done. Another reason that these Priests didn't hold the same honor to God was because those that stood in the office were there out of political needs and weren't descendants of Aaron. They were of the Sadducee and Pharisee groups that held political and financial prowess in the city of Jerusalem. An important lesson to take away is simply this: where there's no history, there will be no honor, adoration, appreciation, or even respect.

The Priests during this time, although they knew the law, taught the law, and even upheld the law of Moses, their hearts were far from Him and they acted out of greed and power. We see these same power driven people accuse and eventually send our Savior Jesus to the cross. But before we get there, let's see what the Word tells us about this priesthood.

Matthew 2:4–6 shows us that the Priests were still the go to people when anyone wanted to know what the Lord had given to the people previously and specifically here, of where Jesus (the Messiah) would be born. There is one exception to these politically and power driven Priests, and his name was Zacharias. Zacharias was a Priest during that time and along with his wife Elizabeth (who was a descendant of Aaron), lived righteous lives before God walking in His commandments and ordinances blame-lessly (Luke 1:6). This is important because this same Priest was sent into the temple to burn incense for the Lord, per his office duties, and was visited by an angel, later revealed to be Gabriel, saying that the Lord had heard his and his wife's prayer of having a child (Luke 1:8–13) and would be the first person in the New Testament to be filled with Holy Spirit.

Now, if you're following along Zacharias is the first person in 400 years to have any heavenly or divine encounter from God. What's inter-esting is from this encounter, Zacharias didn't speak again until his son was born and they named him John. John would go on to be what the Prophet Malachi prophesied that Elijah would come again before the Lord and turn the hearts of the fathers back to the sons (Malachi 4:5–6). Back to Zacharias; after his mouth was opened, he praised God and became filled with Holy Spirit. He prophesied that the Messiah was coming from the line of David and that He would restore the covenant between God and man. He also prophesied to baby John that he was a Prophet, that would prepare the way before Jesus would come on the scene, by calling people to salvation through repentance (Luke 1:57–78).

From Zacharias's life we see that Priests that live righteous lives devoted to God are given the opportunity to encounter Him and speak for Him. Think it not strange that God chose a Priest to bear the seed of a prophet that would prepare the way for our Savior. But still, that's not till later. In my personal opinion I believe God chose Zacharias and his wife specifically to steward the life of John the Baptist based off his duties and life as a true Priest. Now, our faith isn't based on works at all, but God, in all His knowledge, knew that Zacharias's heart was tender toward Him, and because of this he could cultivate a child that would seem "awkward" to the outside world. Let that be a note to parents who read this and have been frustrated with your child because they're not like others. You're right!! And because you're right, you need to seek the Lord for how to raise your child/children because they're set apart for the glory of the Kingdom. Generations to come are a reflection of what they did and didn't learn, but let's stay focused on the task.

The next time we see the priesthood is when the Bible states that Annas and Caiaphas were the High Priests at the time. Annas was the High Priest, then was removed by the Romans, so Caiaphas took his place. These two are pivotal because near the end of Jesus's ministry, they both encountered Him when the Pharisees and Sadducees brought Him in for trial on the charges of blasphemy by Him saying He was the Son of God. It was Caiaphas that plotted to kill Jesus (Matt. 26:3–4, charged Him with blasphemy (Matt. 26:63–66), and that brought Him before Pilate to be sentenced to crucifixion (John 18:28–32). Besides them, we also see that Priests were still the ones to say if someone was clean or not when Jesus healed a man of leprosy and told him to show himself to the Priests (Luke 5:12–14).

All in all, we can say that the Priesthood during Jesus's time was hypocritical (Matthew 6:1–4), lived according to influence and power (John 2:13–17), and held traditions as sacred more than God Himself (Mark 3:2–6). The priesthood of this time was the opposite of what God intended, and because of this, the society suffered greatly for it. As we stated in "Priests of Old," Priests are who remind the nation of God's goodness and help them to remember Him in everything that they do. When a nation doesn't remember what God has done, other gods take His place and let the people do what they think is right, which will lead to death (Proverbs 14:12).

Doesn't this sound familiar today? Where are those that will stand and proclaim what the Lord has done and live according to His standard? I'm hoping this is you who is reading this right now. Although it was the Priests and other religious leaders who sent Jesus to the cross, this term of priesthood is restored by Him as well. Everyone knows the verse in 1 Peter 2:9, "But you are a chosen race, a royal Priesthood, a holy nation, a people for his own possession, that you may proclaim the excellencies of him who called you out of darkness into his marvelous light," but it's before this verse and after that excites me.

Verses 4–8 speaks of how Jesus is the stone that the builders rejected and how those who believe in Him are being built up into spiritual houses for a Holy and dedicated PRIESTHOOD. And it's the verses after 9, specifically 10–12, that show us how to live our lives as this priesthood mentioned, so that the unbeliever may come to glorify God. This is the whole point of this book being written. If I wanted to, I could conclude off those nine verses alone, but because I'm not cruel and want "to present" as much evidence as possible, I'll go further. The purpose of us living as this royal priesthood is so that others can see God in and through us, by our actions, in both public and private, and by the way we speak. Our lives are built on us being servants to God, and by this being our motivation, it rubs off on whoever we're near.

To make this perfectly clear, if you're a new believer, then you're called to this priesthood. Reason being is because when Jesus gave up His spirit on the cross, the veil in the temple was torn from the top to the bottom (Matthew 27:50–51), and the veil represented the divide between man and God due to the fall in the garden (Genesis 3:1–8). It is only through Jesus that we're able to be a part of this priesthood and go before the throne of grace boldly.

If you remember what I explained before in the previous chapter, the Priests were the only ones who were able to go beyond the veil to sacrifice on behalf of the nation. So, because of Jesus's blood being spilled, we don't need the sacrifices anymore, nor do we need Priests to pray on our behalf. Isn't it a beautiful thing that we don't have to have another person to go to God for us but we can do it ourselves?

Jesus's sacrifice also caused us to be joint heirs with Him as children of God who are adopted into the royal family (Romans 8:14–17) by us accepting Him as Lord and believing that He died for our sins. We owe it all to Jesus and because of this, and my love for Him, this next chapter will focus on Him solely as our Savior and High Priest.

OUR HIGH PRIEST

"For such an high priest became us, who is holy, harmless, undefiled, separate from sinners, and made higher than the heavens; Who needeth not daily, as those high priests, to offer up sacrifice, first for his own sins, and then for the people's: for this he did once, when he offered up himself."

- Hebrews 7:26–27 KJV

Jesus is the reason we believe. He is the reason that we give grace to others because He gave grace to us when we didn't deserve it! Romans 5:8 says it like this, "But God demonstrates his own love for us in this. While we were yet sinners, Christ died for us." It was out of God's love and Jesus's love for us that we're able to stand before our God at times dirty, confused, broken hearted, etc. and He hears us. John 15:13 says "No one has greater love [nor stronger commitment] than to lay down his own life for his friends." This is exactly what Jesus showed us by staying on the cross, which brings us to the significance of Him being our High Priest.

The High Priest's main role was on the day of atonement to sacrifice the sacrifices and sprinkle blood on the mercy seat so our sins can be atoned for and forgiven (Leviticus 16:14–16). Besides the day of atonement, they also were the main leaders over the rest of the Priests to ensure that duties were attended to and were the only ones who would wear the Urim and the Thummim, which were used to determine God's will (Numbers 27:21). Jesus accomplished this by: 1) Preaching a message of repentance and salvation to rally and renew the minds of those who would hear Him so His message could prune and purify them (John 15:3), 2) The day on Golgotha's hill, His body was given as a sacrifice for the entire world and His blood was spilled for atonement, and 3) Him being the Messiah makes Him the head of us which are the church. Which is an interesting dichotomy because the High Priests were those who usually killed the sacrifice, then came out to announce what the Lord had stated over the nation, but now we see that in one moment, our Savior is both the Priest and sacrifice.

Jesus's message is of love to the world and retells a story of how God desires to be in relationship with us directly. His role of High Priest comes in when He keeps Himself on the cross so His blood as the lamb can be spilled to atone and break the curse of sin forever! Isn't that good news?! Think about it, Jesus laid down His life out of love so we might choose Him, emphasis on might. Jesus knew it wasn't a guarantee that we would choose Him, but knew that with His death what was guaranteed was freedom from sin. Love doesn't count up the cost, but it bears all things, believes all things, hopes for all things, and endures all things (1 Cor. 13:7).

I emphasized Jesus's death being an atonement because as we've spoken from the Old Testament to the new, the importance of blood being spilled was for God's mercy and grace to be poured out and as a means of worship to Him. Jesus knew this because He was there in the beginning and helped establish all that we know, so for Him to become that for us meant He understood this was the only way to reconcile us to the Father. And by Him rising means that all those who accept Him as Lord are buried and raised with Him to have victory over sin, hell, and the grave as new creatures (Romans 6:4). Him being our High Priest means that He is our go to; and example. He's pleading on our behalf to God at His right hand.

The Bible says it like this, "Who then can say we are guilty? It was Christ Jesus Who died. He was raised from the dead. He is on the right side of God praying to Him for us" (Romans 8:34).

Also, Him being our High Priest proves Him true when He said that He is the way, the truth, and the life, and no one can get to the Father but through Him (John 14:6). That's the spitting image of the High Priests duty to God and the nation to act as a bridge or messenger. We as the royal priesthood, take our commands from Jesus and how He trained His disciples, how He lived His own life, and even Him laying His life down for the sake of doing God's will. That's the true testament of a Priest outside of their duty. Would you die for God's will to be done? Would you give your life for this Gospel? These are sobering and important questions to ask ourselves while being a perfect segway into the next chapter.

PRACTICALITY TO THE PRIESTHOOD

"And you and your sons with you shall guard your priesthood for all that concerns the altar and that is within the veil; and you shall serve. I give your priesthood as a gift, and any outsider who comes near shall be put to death."
- Numbers 18:7 ESV

Now that we have the history behind the priesthood, the why and necessity of it, and who our example is, now look at Jesus's life as well as the lives of the New Testament believers for practical wisdom. I believe we have to deal with whether we truly believe that Jesus is who He is first. Reason being, if He's not solely who we believe in then we can't truly be the royal priesthood; not because we're not, but due to the conflicting beliefs in our minds and hearts. Part of the reason the Priests of old diverted from God was because in their hearts, they weren't submitted. They blessed Him with their mouths but their hearts were far from Him (Isaiah 29:13, Ezekiel 33:31, Matthew 15:7–9).

Those are three different scriptures around the same subject because this was a reality of the people and the Priests, which is why if Jesus isn't who we truly believe in, then we'll follow our feelings and base our theology off what feels good or what we think is best, which leads to death (Proverbs 14:12). A healthy doing of this will cause our faith to rise as well as prompt us to do deep dives into questions that may arise. The great thing about following Jesus is He welcomes our questions! Proverbs 4:7 says in all thy getting, get wisdom. I believe we can't get wisdom if we don't ask questions. This may introduce some to what is called Apologetics, in which you learn to defend the scriptures by knowing historical facts mixed with biblical contexts. In my opinion, all believers should be able to defend their faith against atheists, Buddhists, Muslims, Hinduists, witchcraft, new age, etc. This world is searching for truth and we have access to that truth.

So, **step 1 is to believe that Jesus is the son of God and our Savior**, which will lead us into the next step. **Step 2: Study the word and pray**. This seems elementary but this is what sets our foundation and keeps our feelings and thoughts from ruling our lives. As mentioned, before Priests were the holders, teachers, and examples of the law in the Old Testament. Now, since we're under the new covenant, which is God's promise to forgive all sins of those who turn their hearts over to Him through Jesus, those duties of teaching and being examples still apply. We as Priests need to know what the Bible says so we can not only live it out but teach others to do the same and bring people to Christ through the Gospel.

Jesus Himself is a perfect example of this because He's who taught the Apostles (or disciples) and the congregations that followed the principle of the Kingdom of God. They often referred to Him as Rabbi or teacher because He showed them revelatory things about the word of God and how God's Kingdom showed these principles. After Jesus rose and spent some time with the disciples, He instructed them to go make disciples and teach them what He had taught them (Matthew 28:19–20), which to me, speaks of the High Priest instructing the Priests under Him what to do.

How should this be done? I suggest starting off with 20 to 30 minutes of prayer, worship, and study, specifically with the four Gospels, Matthew, Mark, Luke, and John, then branch out from there. Pray and ask God to reveal Himself through the scriptures and to invite Him into wherever you are. Don't be alarmed if this turns into you singing songs, walking, rocking back and forth, or even crying. This will build relationship and intimacy so He can speak to your heart.

The reason I say study the Gospels first is because the entire sixty-six books are about Jesus and if we're able to understand Him and His life while He was physically here on Earth, we'll see the old and new route its way back to Him. It's like a tree; every leaf comes from a branch, every branch is connected to a trunk, and that trunk is supported and nourished by roots, which are within a solid foundation. Jesus is that firm foundation (Ephesians 2:19–22) that we should build all of our belief, thoughts, and activities around. This doesn't mean you don't go to parties, can't listen to music other than Gospel, or even look good but this does mean the fact that we proclaim Jesus should always take precedence over everything we do. Don't be too heavenly conscious that you're no earthly good.

Step 3: Apply what you're studying to your daily living. The entire book of James is rich on the subject of living Holy and sanctified but if I could sum it up, it would be, practice what you preach. The Apostle James, who is Jesus's half brother, instructs us Christians to live out what we're reading because it causes our lives to change and reflect Jesus. Faith applied is what changes lives. Why is living this life important though? Why can't we believe in Jesus, know how to pray, and know what the Bible says? Why isn't that enough?! I'm glad you asked and I believe it's answered in the words Jesus spoke to the disciples. He told them to love each other as He has loved them and by this love shown everyone will know that they're under His leadership (John 13:34–35). We can apply this to us because as believers, as Priests, we're too Jesus's disciples, and the way we add to the Kingdom is by knowing the Word and loving others.

Step 4: Find community and talk through what you're learning. This is a very key part in the practical guide because from the beginning, the Lord said it wasn't good for man to be alone. We were made to be in fellowship and community! Community will help keep us accountable, troubleshoot any issues we're having, help us learn the word, and even challenge our thinking when it comes to scripture, as well as topics that arise in our lives. The Priests and Prophets of old used this same method where there were schools of the Prophets (1 Samuel 19:18–24, 2 Kings 2 and 4:38–44) as well as Jesus with His disciples, so we could call this a principle of faith. Priests should always be in community because it helps our growth and urges us to go deeper!

Step 5: Teach others and repeat. These are very practical steps that will influence our natural lives, as well as our spiritual lives to live as the royal priesthood we've been called to be! It's a privilege to be a Priest and it's a sacred position that God has given us the responsibility to handle. These steps carried out may look different for everyone but at the core of them should be the intent of growing closer to God, showing the world Jesus, and winning souls for the Kingdom. Now that we've hit on the practicality, let's hit some of the dangers Priests run into. The first is the trading of God's opinion because of the fear of man. This is dangerous because the fear of man's word will cause us to question what God has said which will then lead us to follow what man thinks is good.

By now, a scripture should've popped back up in your head (hint: it's earlier in the chapter). Aaron's example of this in Exodus 32 is while Moses was on the mountain, Aaron built a golden calf out of fear of what the people would do. This led them to worship gods of Egypt rather than the God who brought them out of bondage. If you read further, God instructed Moses to go down and get the people in order because He was going to unleash His wrath on them, but Moses speaks to God on the behalf of the people so they could be spared and it was so. Priests, we have to stay planted in what God says and trust that Holy Spirit is leading us correctly. If we don't, we will lead a group, a people, a nation into false worship. Our duty to be the spokesperson for the people is crucial because as you read in the chapter, it can cause God's grace to pour out on who we pray for. Jesus is doing it for us at the right hand of the Father, so we should do it for others!

Another danger is the temptation to self-medicate to deal with our issues. What that means is we take it into our own hands to please ourselves. Examples of this could look like using drugs or alcohol to have peace, using sex or masturbation to fill a void, etc. These cause us to forsake God's presence and our victory in Jesus. We have to remember that it's in God's presence that we receive our peace, our strength, and our joy and we can cast our cares on Him (1 Peter 5:7). The amplified version says it like this, "casting all your cares [all your anxieties, all your worries, and all your concerns, once and for all] on Him, for He cares about you [with deepest affection, and watches over you very carefully]." We know who we can turn to and that He renews our strength.

Lastly, another danger is becoming power hungry. One example of many is what we mentioned in chapter 2 about Eli's sons. They were the Priests in the temple and because they knew the people had to come to them they were taking advantage of them and having sex with the Levite women in the temple. Bringing that into modern day this could look like manipulating those we serve into doing things we want them to do rather than leading them closer to Jesus. This is detrimental because outside of us not acting like Jesus, we damage people. Damaging people with our influence causes them to stray from and have nothing to do with God which we now know as church hurt.

Can I suggest that church hurt didn't come from God, but from a supposed follower of Christ not resembling Him who took advantage of somebody not knowing any better? This is why the position of the Priest was created, so we could help people steward and grow their relationship with God! I started the book stating that we're called to SERVE; how can we do that if we're damaging the people we're supposed to serve? With that being said, let's go forth and be the Priests God has called us to be. Let's be those set apart for the glory of God in order to bring that glory to those who are in need of their spirit man coming alive. Let's be those who represent Jesus and invite others to know Him. Let's be those who protect and steward the altar, so what's being presented is pure and of our Father. Priests, we have a duty to serve the people and bring them into the presence of God. Take up your position and steward it well! You are a royal Priesthood and a child of God. Let's act like it and go forth. Let me pray over you. Stay tuned for the bonus chapter too!

Practical Steps:

1. Believe Jesus is the son of God and your Savior.

2. Study the word and pray.

3. Apply what you're studying to your daily life.

4. Find community and talk through what you're learning.

5. Teach others and repeat.

Heavenly Father, we come now to say thank you. We thank you for life and we thank you for the breath that's in our lungs. It's with this breath that we're alive in you Jesus and it's that same breath that we give back to you in our worship. We're honored to be a chosen people and to be set apart for your purpose and glory, and we pray that your glory will be manifested through us as we serve you and your people. I pray now, in the name of Jesus, for the man or woman's spirit reading this book to come alive! May the refreshing and restoration of your presence surround them now. I pray that the weight of your glory would bring them to their knees in honor and adoration, to you our king. May you purify their hearts, so as they take up this mantle of a Priest, that they wouldn't sin against you or mislead your people. May this Priest not only move and speak with integrity, but will be bold and courageous. May they hear the words that you spoke to Jeremiah in telling him not to be afraid of their faces because you're with them to protect and deliver them. We will stand as the Priests of your temple and teach them your ways. We will stand as your Priests and lead them into worship. We will stand as your Priests and guide them to your presence. We will pursue you with reckless abandon because we love and adore you. Now Father, I bless them in their coming and going. May your favor be upon them and your face toward them. In Jesus's name I pray. Amen!

BONUS

■ ■ ■

PRIESTS AND THE PROPHETIC

"Then I fell down at his feet to worship him, but he [stopped me and] said to me, "You must not do that; I am a fellow servant with you and your brothers and sisters who have and hold the testimony of Jesus. Worship God [alone]. For the testimony of Jesus is the spirit of prophecy [His life and teaching are the heart of prophecy]."

- Revelations 19:10 AMP

Remember in the earlier chapter, I mentioned that there were a couple of Priests that too were Prophets? Reference the end of "Old Testament Priests." The reason I mentioned this is because Priests and Prophets are vastly similar as much as they are different. Their main difference is one speaks on the behalf of the people (Priests) and the other speaks on the behalf of God (Prophets). But the common interest is that both love God immensely, have a mandate to Him, and steward the people to follow His ways. I wholeheartedly believe that the hearts of Priests and Prophets are so similar for the reasons above and because they're both used to be bridges between the natural and supernatural.

What I mean by this is simply that both have to hear in order to go from one of these realms to the other with information that will be distributed in order to produce change. It's this change that is the catalyst for pulling God's will to Earth so that His kingdom can be established. Before I go further, let me explain what prophecy is and what it isn't. Prophecy is simply God's message to the Earth. To dig a bit deeper, it's the translation of His heart and mind to all mankind so we can know Him and be led by Him. Prophecy is as old as time itself because it stays true to what we've used to define it.

We see God speaking to Adam on what to do in order to cultivate the garden, as well as to both Cain and Abel. Let me plow right here for a little bit because I sense that someone will read this and scrunch their faces reading that last sentence. Yes, God spoke to Cain too! But it wasn't because God was pleased with Cain, it was to tell Cain that the Earth groaned to Him because Abel's blood cried out from the ground and that he was cursed to be a nomad the rest of his life (Gen. 4:10–13). This lets us know that God doesn't only speak to the good things or good people, but to the opposite as well if that means His will is done, which will produce change and offer them the direct opportunity to be saved.

Prophecy is one of God's tools to change the Earth through people which brings us back to the importance and identicalness of the Priest and Prophet. Priests, whose hearts long for God, will be naturally prophetic because they're adoration will bring them before Him and He will speak to them, whether it's specifically for them, for another person, etc. This is why we often see that those with the grace or heart of a Priest are often in positions where they have to communicate and get a message across. Notice how I just said that they're in positions that call them to communicate, which is where the cross-reference between the Priest and Prophet connect, like I mentioned earlier. This is also where the Priest communicates God's will and way, from the Word but can tap into the mind/heart of God if He has something specific to say.

I would name some positions or people with titles that would fit these descriptions, but as we've already stated the royal priesthood is the body of Christ! The entire body of Christ are Priests and as Joel stated in 2:28 and Peter said in Acts 2:17–18, God is pouring out His spirit on us so that we all may prophesy! Prophecy is for every believer and is accessible to those that believe, but it has to be stewarded correctly. Free prophetic training: every word that you believe is from God should mirror His character, lead back to scripture, and lead people to follow Jesus or lead them to act more like Him. Another freebie: the prophetic cannot be controlled because it doesn't come from us, but it's from Holy Spirit, (2 Peter 1:21), Holy Spirit, by way of Jesus, is our bridge between the natural and supernatural and because He is from God, He can search the depths of God and deliver what He finds to us.

I have receipts! 1 Corinthians 2:10–13 speaks of how Holy Spirit takes information that He finds about God and shares the revelation with us so we can know more about God. From this information, we can agree that all those who believe and accept Jesus can receive Holy Spirit, which then gives them an open door to walk in the prophetic. Let me give a few examples of those who walked in both offices: Samuel, Jeremiah, and Ezekiel. All three performed Priestly duties, but from birth, were called by God as Prophets. Reading their books in the Bible lets us in on their devotion to God and establishing His ways among the nation of Israel. This emphasizes our duty as New Covenant believers that our devotion should, like them, but more importantly, Jesus, be to love God with all of our hearts, love our neighbors like ourselves, and push the Kingdom further through the spreading of the Gospel. Priests, keep your hearts, minds, ears, and eyes open and allow Holy Spirit to download revelation to you so more souls can be saved, believers equipped to do the same, and continue to build the Kingdom up.

www.ingramcontent.com/pod-product-compliance
Lightning Source LLC
Chambersburg PA
CBHW050444150626
46551CB00028B/1565